Mounting & Framing Pictures

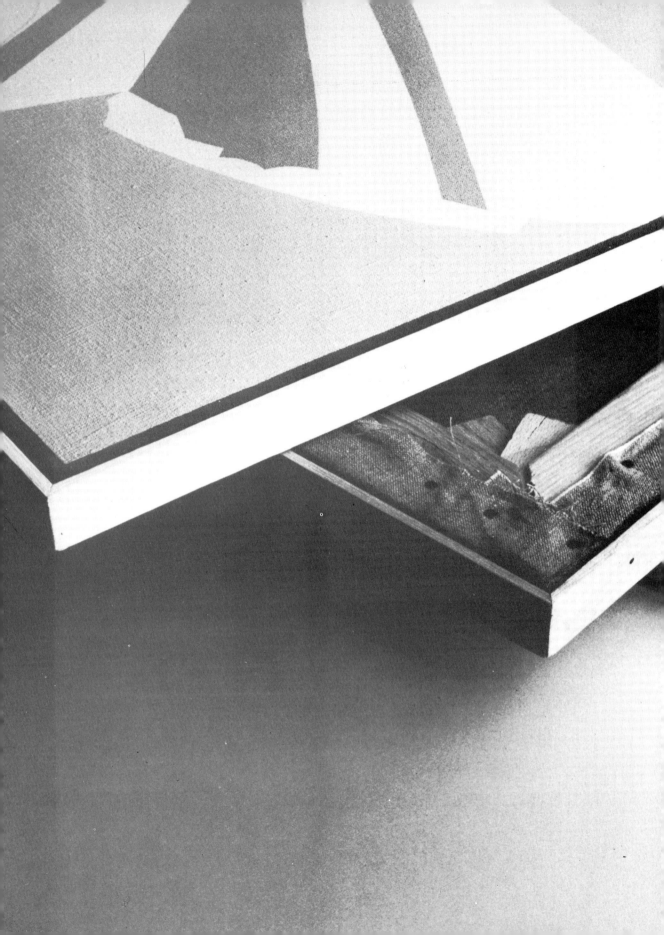

Mounting & Framing Pictures

Michael Woods

B T Batsford Limited London

Dedicated to my Father, Reginald Woods, M.B.E., who first
encouraged my use of his workshop

Book design by Alphabet and Image,
Sherborne, Dorset
Designer: Jamie Hobson

First published 1978
First published in paperback 1981
Reprinted 1982, 1984
ISBN 0 7134 0744 1 (paperback)

Printed and bound in Great Britain by
Anchor Brendon Ltd
Tiptree, Essex
for the publishers
B T Batsford Limited
4 Fitzhardinge Street
London W1H 0AH

Contents

Introduction

It is a magic moment to hang a picture on a wall. Suddenly the wall becomes relatively unimportant and it can seem as if a new window has been let into it. It might be a reminder of a most happy holiday — a print full of colour, or a treasured find from a market stall. No matter what it is, it will be special and important to you.

Yet all too frequently those feelings and the enjoyment of looking and looking over the months ahead are limited to only one or two places in a house. Not because pictures are disliked, but for the task, and sometimes the unknown cost, of framing. Yet it is really very simple to mount and frame pictures.

Probably one particular possession will start you off, but when that has been framed and is proudly on a wall, the fever starts. What else can be framed? There are so many possibilities. Magazines sometimes produce special pages with framing in mind. Embroidered samplers, posters, children's drawings, stamps, illustrations from old and broken books, old postcards, cigarette cards — and yet there are possibilities beyond the two dimensional. Keys and small shells, bits of old watches, buttons and old tools can all be considered.

I shall be discussing hanging pictures in Chapter 7 but when thinking about what you want to do and what to choose, I should certainly make a plea for a wall somewhere in the house which will take eight or twelve small, but all differently framed, pictures or objects. There, on that wall, one by one, can hang your frames. There you can compare and look and have ideas; experiment to find what is best for your pictures, and consider your own likes and dislikes.

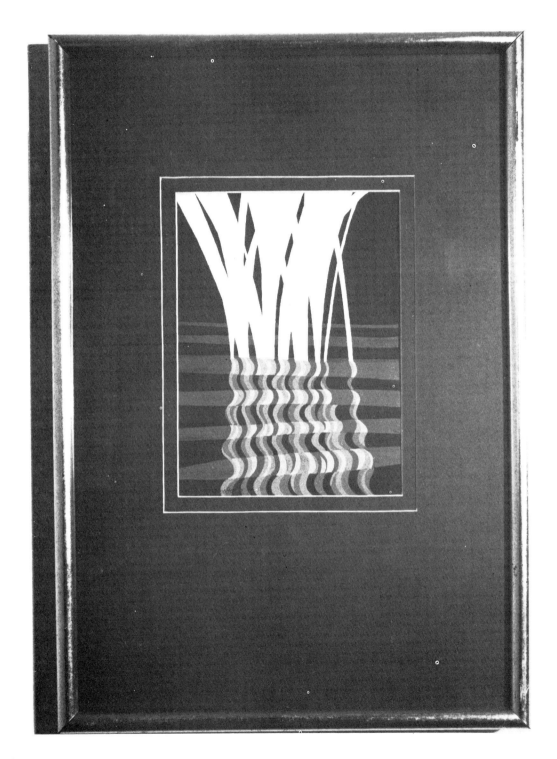

8

1 Types of frame

There are no absolute rules. A good frame is one which you feel complements your picture, but a few guide lines may be helpful.

Oil paintings on canvas A simple batten will not cover any of the picture. A frame with a rabbet should only cover as much of the picture as is needed to hold it in place. The width of a frame with moulding wants to look generous enough — too thin and it will appear petty. It is better to have a single thin edge if you cannot use a generous moulding.

Left: A framed water colour.
Below: An example of a simple but effective batten framing an oil painting.

Michael Woods 3-6-73 the Vanbrugh bridge at Blenheim.

Michael Woods 3-6-73 the Vanbrugh bridge at Blenheim.

Water colours Traditionally the water colour frame is a thin one and extra size made up by the mount. If the edge of the water colour is not covered by the mount the work will look lighter, freer, possibly more vigorous, but not so realistic; the random edge will show the paint quality. If the mount covers the edge, the work will look tighter, less vigorous, but more realistic; the effect of 'the window' onto the view will be increased.

Drawings Should the edge be seen or not — needing the same consideration as water colours. Probably it is a good idea to let the drawing breathe and show every part of it.

Top left: A water colour with random edge showing.
Bottom left: The same water colour with the edge covered.
Top and bottom right: The same effect with a drawing.

Left: A mounted silk screen
Above: An etching with and without the edge showing.
Right: Mounted photograph.

Prints — etchings, silk screen, lithographs
Though you may choose otherwise, the traditional method is to show the edge of the print — in fact it shows the skill of the printmaker and should be crisp anyway. The etching should show the edge of the plate as well, revealed as a round cornered rectangular dent made when the damp paper was pressed onto the plate.

Prints of the mass-produced type can be treated in any manner.

Photographs Best when trimmed — that is no white border round the edge — and mounted onto card using a rubber base glue, or use photographers' dry mounting paper. Generally it is best to show the whole composition letting the actual edge of the photograph be seen.

Three dimensional objects The frame is virtually a setting for the object or group of objects which will be fixed to a plain centre panel. The frame will have to have sufficient depth to accommodate the objects if glass is incorporated in its design.

2 The work area

It can be only the reader who will know the room in which work can take place. The possibilities are so varied that to list them would only serve to bore those who know quite well where they can work. Still, frame making can be undertaken by anybody who might not normally have a work room. It is not a dirty occupation — sawdust is easily swept up and most frames will lie on an opened-out newspaper. So what qualities are important? Uncut lengths of wood at the start can be very long, so a small room with a well-placed door or

Below: It is not advisable to use the dining table as a work area unless it is well protected.

window will give a chance for the first cuts to be made. A sturdy table is most important, and must be one on which a vice can be clamped. Small mobile work benches might serve, though there is a great calmness gained by being able to spread out all the materials on a good large, rectangular table, say 1.5 m x 1.2 m (5 ft x 4 ft). The surface should be as flat as possible, with no joints, for any cracks and waves in the surface can make simple jobs difficult.

If you do have to cover a table with a work-on-able sheet of material, choose a sheet of compressed chipboard with some old material stuck on the back to prevent scratching, and devise an edge to overlap and locate the temporary top on the resident table to prevent it shifting.

A shelf in easy reach nearby, or another small table at about the same height as the main table, is also invaluable — a mobile kitchen trolley would be ideal — enabling tools to be kept at hand but away from the actual work.

Top left: A kitchen trolley is an ideal accessory.
Left: An angle poise lamp firmly clamped to the work table.
Right: Necessary tools. From the top: pliers, hammer and pins, set squares, bradawl, hand drill and bits, knife, tenon saw and mitre box.

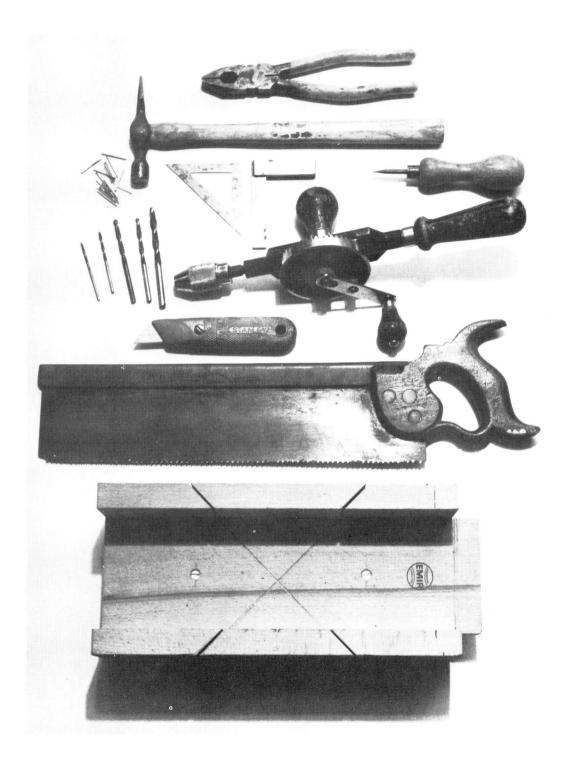

3 Mounts

A mount is a surround to a drawing which gives it space to breathe; an area of calm to help focus on the work itself. The usual mount is made of a special card — stiff and thick, yet easily cuttable. But one does not necessarily have to use this special material to greatly improve a drawing. Many people produce work in quantity, and to frame just one piece for all time is hardly sensible, so try the following treatment.

Trim the drawing to a crisp rectangle. Cut off drawing pin holes and bent over corners. Clean up any easily removed, unwanted marks — possibly re-sign and date the work closer in to the drawing if it is yours, or get the artist to do so — don't forge the signature! Lay the drawing on a sheet of paper: sugar paper, cover paper; shops may just call it coloured paper. Use what you can get of a colour you like; plain white paper can look well. I will assume that you have a frame in mind — possibly that you will use one of the frames described in Chapter 4. If the drawing is on an A2 sheet then an A2 size frame will be about right. In practice I would guess that you will have trimmed about 50 mm (2 in.) off each side, so when the drawing is placed back on to an A2 sheet there will be a border of about 50 mm (2 in.). With two tiny pieces of self-adhesive putty, one at each top corner, place the drawing down onto the backing paper. Check that the picture is centrally placed — if any extra space is available keep the bottom of the border the largest. With a soft lead pencil and ruler, mark out and draw a single pencil line on the backing paper, about 10 mm (3/8 in.) from the drawing edge. This sounds simple and it is, but it is surprising how effective it can be, and if using the same frame you wish to change the drawing and have a different border, it will only take fifteen minutes to do so. This paper border is ideal when used in conjunction with the 'no frame frame' described on page 55. If a traditional section frame is used, it is possible to fix turning clips at the back, making access very much quicker. The cut mount involves the same questions of size, proportion and colour, but gives a more permanent and considerably richer feeling because of the thickness of the mounting card which is revealed when it is cut with a bevelled edge.

The card is made in a wide range of colours and though not all small art shops will stock a big range, a little searching will probably provide the colour that is right for you. But what is right? Test the colours against the picture. Make a collection of samples. Pieces of old mounting card, card painted with samples of emulsion

Left: Two 'L' shaped pieces of card used to determine the mount size.
Fig. 1: Mount showing marking points well away from the corners of the rectangle to be cut.
Bottom right: When marking the card prior to cutting it is important to avoid denting it.

paint, pieces of wrapping paper, cuttings from cardboard boxes — the wider the range of samples the better.

Four 100 mm (4 in.) strips 600 mm (2 ft long) will be most helpful, for when layed round the picture an immediate, if rough, idea of colour will be obtained. Though light, off white, colours can be bright and fresh, they do not show off some pale water colours well, and it is worth trying dark tones, a holly green, or a dark sepia brown, or a gunmetal grey — they can look very rich. But the walls against which they are to hang must be taken into account, for though the picture is of course very important, it is the relationship of colour, tone, size and lighting which in the end will make the framing look tired or alive.

The item to be mounted must be considered very carefully, taking into account the points made in Chapter 1. Two L-shaped pieces of mounting card are very useful to determine the exact picture area wanted, which will be the same as the rectangle to be cut in the mount. Write this size down. To each of the two dimensions add 200 mm (8 in.), ie a picture size seen 250 mm x 500 mm (10 in. x 20 in.) will require a piece of mounting card 250 + 200 x 500 + 200 = 450 mm x 700 mm (10 + 8 x 20 + 8 = 18 in. x 28 in.).

Consider the most economical marking out of this on your whole sheet of mounting card and mark it out with care. The card to be cut should lay on your smooth, clean and flat table and with your knife cut off the piece you have marked. Now refresh your memory as to the dimensions you require and, well away from the corners of the mount you are to cut, mark the sides on the seen face. You may wish all four

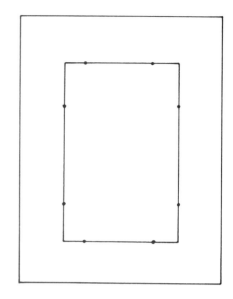

Fig. 1

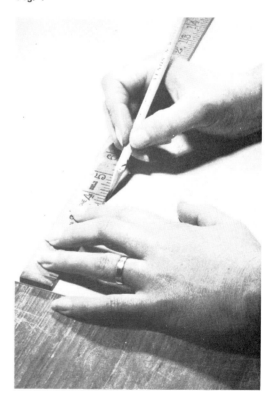

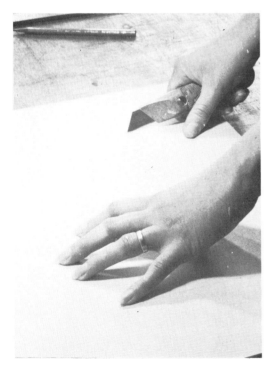

sides to be the same, in which case mark the top and bottom as well, but I recommend for a more 'comfortable' position you allow 95 mm (3¾ in.) at the top and 105 mm (4¼ in.) at the bottom. Because the marking has to be done on the actual face of the mounting card, care must be taken not to put the dots for the lines beyond where the lines will go. Do not overshoot the corners, for a pencil will actually dent mounting card and rubbing out will not only mar the surface but it will not remove the dent.

With nothing in the way behind you, and with a brand new blade in your knife, hold it, leaning over to the right if you are right-handed, at approximately 45° to the surface of the card. The tip of the blade should lie just to the right, or outside edge, of the line so that you can see it as you cut. Get your light adjusted. The line itself will be left on the centre piece which is being removed. Lean forward but be prepared to move your body backwards, without moving your feet. Make an incision, right through the thickness of the card — you only want to cut once — and then keeping your arm tense, draw the whole of your body backwards and cut down the length of the line to the corner. Take the knife out. Turn the card through 90° anticlockwise so that you prepare to continue the cut down the next side, following the first. Make the incision and drawing your body and arm back together, make the second cut — all the time keeping your eye on the pencil line. In a similar fashion cut the third and fourth sides, finally returning to the corner of starting. It is unlikely that the centre piece will immediately drop out, for almost certainly little pieces of card will remain uncut just at the corners. So, with great care to re-enter the cut at exactly the same angle with the knife, hold the mounting card in the air and recut the corner both ways into the corner. You will suddenly feel the mount free. Repeat with the three other corners and the centre should be free to remove. The card edge will be very sharp, sharp

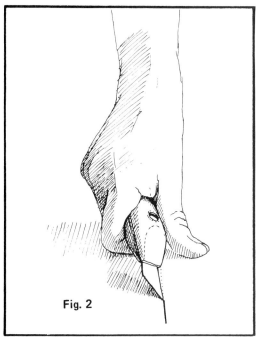

enough to cut your finger, so take care, but any slight whiskers of paper are best pressed down, or back and under rather than trying to cut them off — you will only damage the crisp edge of your cut if you do try to cut them. Then with your picture lying flat on the table, try the mount on it.

Fig. 2

Top left and Fig. 2: Mount cutting showing the large handled knife and the holding angle.
Bottom left and Fig. 3: The position of the thumb running on the card surface should be noted.

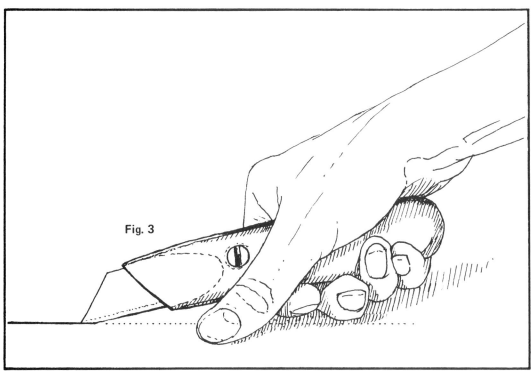

Fig. 3

There are various methods of fixing the drawing to the mount.

Method 1 Place the drawing face down on a clean surface, glass or a plastic surface is best. Along the top edge lightly stick a length of masking tape 15 mm (½ in.) wide (not transparent adhesive tape, it sticks too well and stains and becomes brittle in time). Overlap the top by half the width of the tape.

Turn the drawing over (the overlap bit will unpeel from the table surface) and hold the mount over the drawing. Without touching the sticky tape, lower the mount, considering just the exact position you wish to place it down. Use your judgement for the right place — pencil marks will rarely be as visually accurate. Place it down and apply a little pressure to make the tape stick. Pick up the mount, the drawing should come with it, but of course it will tend to hinge down. Turn the whole mount over and re-press the tape to the back of the mounting card. If you have a tough piece of paper, with four small pieces of tape, fix it to the mounting card across the back of the drawing, mainly for protection, but use a white piece if your drawing is on white or pale paper, for some paper will show the backing through. The drawing fixed in this way will expand and contract with temperature variations. Fixing all round will only produce wrinkles across its surface.

Method 2 If you have another piece of card, the same size as the outside size of your mount, then this method is preferable. This is also the method used if you wish to simply mount your drawing without framing it. It is used for mounting more valuable works where one would not dream of cutting off any pieces of paper, or fixing with anything but the minimum possible. It enables the whole of the paper to be seen, not just the picture, when the mount is lifted.

The backing card and the cut mount are hinged together at the top by means of masking, glue or fabric tape. The mount is then hinged up and the drawing placed on the backing board.

The exact position is found by trial and error and when exactly right, a dampened piece of water gum paper is fixed along the top back of the drawing. This is then folded back to form a hinge, which is then stuck to the backing card. Something as little as 3 mm (⅛ in.) will be enough to just hold the work. If you wish of course masking tape can be used here if it will do no harm, and this can be used as a hinge or simply flat in the cases where there is a lot of spare paper beyond the work itself.

Facing page:—
Top left: Re-entering the cut mount to free a corner.
Top right: Trying the mount on the drawing.
Bottom left: Taping the top of the mount and drawing.
Bottom right: Smoothing the tape at the back.
Below: The hinged mount, open.

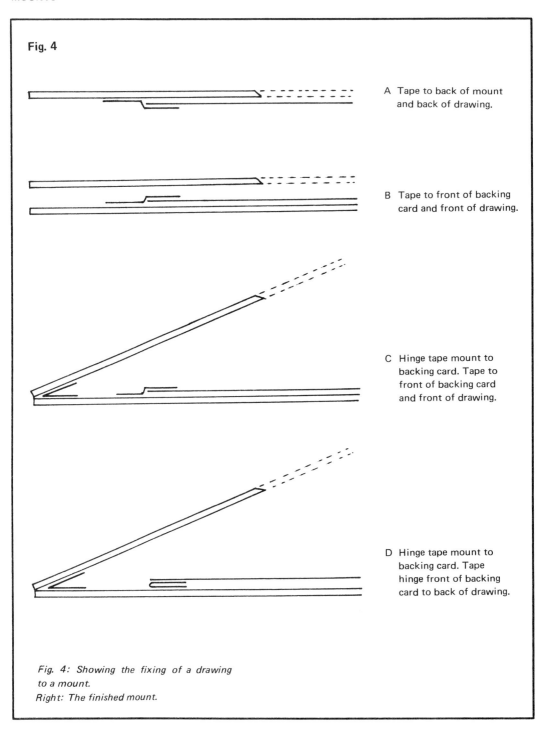

Fig. 4

A Tape to back of mount and back of drawing.

B Tape to front of backing card and front of drawing.

C Hinge tape mount to backing card. Tape to front of backing card and front of drawing.

D Hinge tape mount to backing card. Tape hinge front of backing card to back of drawing.

Fig. 4: Showing the fixing of a drawing to a mount.
Right: The finished mount.

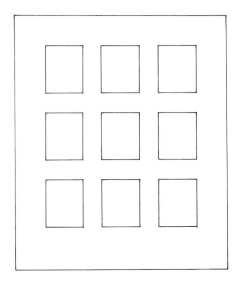

Fig. 5

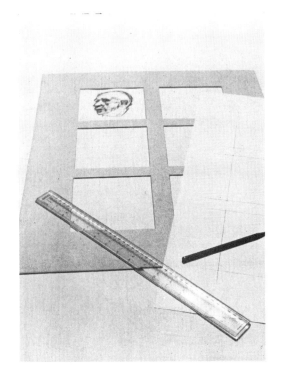

With small drawings it can be quite effective to cut a mount with more than one apperture. Two, three, four, six, eight can be happily mounted together. Of course the planning and laying out will be more complicated, but work the whole layout to the exact size on a sheet of paper first. It will not matter how many adjustments or wrong marks are made. When the run through is complete, and exact, cut the paper to the outside size that you will require your mounting card. Cut your mounting card to the same size. Lay the paper on top of the mounting card and keep in place with metal clips or little pieces of tape taken over to the back. Then, when it cannot shift, prick through the corners of the rectangles to be cut and into the card. Remove the paper and with a fine pencil connect up the points to make the rectangle. Then cut the bevels as before.

Oval or round mounts can be very attractive if the image is a vignette, ie not a firm rectangle but a shape made of the objects drawn. Portraits are a classic example.

Once again I would plan on paper if the marking out is not straightforward. A compass will give you a circle; two compasses, the pointed end of one fixed where the pencil would be in the other, will give a greater span; a piece of thin cord tied round a pencil and fixed to a drawing pin; or a variety of bowls and plates which by trial and error may have just the right size.

For the oval two drawing pins and a loop of thin string will produce many variations of proportions, but once again a hunt in the kitchen may suddenly produce convenient ovals. Plates and dishes, gravy boat saucers, even an oval frame itself. In this latter case, to obtain a mount size the same proportion as a frame but smaller in the opening size, use a pencil with a spacing piece of wood taped to it. Carefully run this round the inside of the frame, either directly on to the mounting card or on to a piece of tracing paper.

The round or oval mount is cut in the same way as the rectangular sort, but at the end of one part of the curve, as you turn the card and take breath, considerable care will be needed to keep the curve smooth. This will be achieved with a little practice.

Fig. 5: Multi mount.
Bottom left: Multi mount with illustration.
Fig. 6: Marking out an oval.
Top right: A tin lid is useful for marking a circle.
Bottom right: Marking a circular or oval frame with a pencil and piece of wood for spacing.

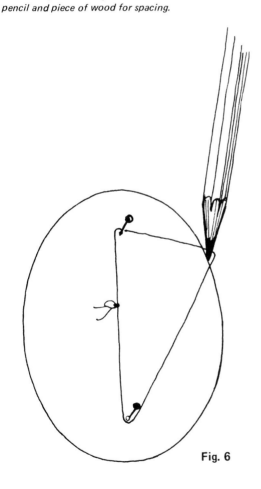

Fig. 6

MOUNTS

A method of giving an extra richness to a work is to use two mounts. The second mount cut, say, 20 mm (¾ in.) bigger than the first, thus mounting the mount. The same colour card or a different colour can be used but it will be the bevel edge of the mount which will create the lines round the drawing. This is the elaborate version of the pencil line used in the simple mount on page 19.

Pale mounts can be given an extra richness by lines drawn round the opening. Ruling pens using water colour are used to create the lines, greys and sepia being more gentle than full black. The availability of the draughtsman's stilo tipped pen greatly facilitates the ruling of lines — they are easy to use and do not blot. The wash, again of water colour, is laid between lines with a brush of exactly the same working width. Experiment and practice is needed for these operations and for certain mounts and pictures the appearance is worth the effort.

A simple marking device is made by cutting a strip of card with a 45° angle. Along the angle marks are made at 3 mm (⅛ in.) intervals. These can be selected for the spaces required and repeated at each corner very quickly and accurately, with either a pin prick or the tiniest pencil dot.

Top right: A double mount.
Bottom right: Marking the corner.
Facing page:—
Top left: Joining the corners with a Rotring pen.
Top right: Practise laying the wash on an odd piece of card.
Below: Finished mount with wash lines.

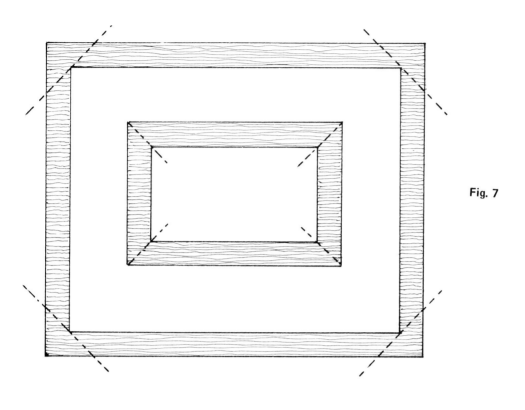

Fig. 7

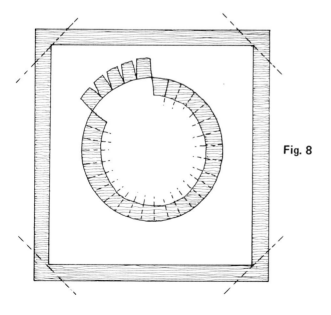

Fig. 8

Fig. 7: Covering a mount. The dotted
lines are the cutting lines after the face
has been stuck down.
Fig. 8: Covering a circular mount.
Right: Making the inside cuts.

The idea of covering a card mount with a piece of material seems a good idea but I have reservations. The material can create too much interest, and the picture can end up being dwarfed by the importance of the mount and frame. From the point of view of room decoration, one might consider the colour of the mount and frame the most important factor. It is, but, and it's a big but, taking due account of the picture itself. It is a mistake to feel that by making everything match, unity will follow. Material falling in folds in curtains will not look the same when stretched over a chair; so too the flat, rectangular nature of a mount, covered by glass, will again look different. So experiment and try alternatives; above all let the drawing or painting remain the most important element. Cut the mount using the method described on page 22. Stretch the material out face down and take care to line up any weave with the lines of the mount which is laid on top of it. Mark round the edges with a soft pencil. Remove the mount and draw the cutting lines across what will become the opening. Mark the

outside corners of the mount area so that when brought round the back of the mount the fabric will just about meet on the corner in a mitre line, that is on the diagonal. The angle to the corner will be 45° to the side. For glue use a weak rubber type glue which is spread very thinly over the face of the mount. Too much and it will stain the material. Lightly and accurately replace the mount down onto the back of the material, lining up on the original pencil marks. Cut out the material with great care at the inside corners, the material must just pull round the thickness of the mount. Fold the material onto the back and mark where it will reach. Place glue on those areas, and working on the inside and outside of one side at a time, press the material onto the glue. A length of wood or an old ruler will help to apply pressure evenly over a long length. As quickly as possible do all four sides. Remove any traces of glue from your fingers and turn the whole mount over. There should be time to tension any of the material on the back to pull out any wrinkles on the front. Stay with the mount while the glue dries. The spring or give in the material will pull on the glue until the moment it is dry enough, and wrinkles can develop.

An oval or circular mount can be covered, but of course many little tabs must be cut to take the material round the back. If material with some stretch in its weave can be chosen, this will be found to stick and mould itself to the curve of the card mount more sympathetically.

A final point. If you intend to mount drawings, using no frames, and have to send them through the post, or are in any way concerned about their safety in travel, use the centre piece of card from each mount and 're-plug' the hole, thus protecting the work. Of course only exactly the same piece must be used, and replaced exactly the same way round as cut. The bevel edge will of course prevent it pressing through, and it will act as a kind of lid.

4 Making the frame

A painting on canvas stretched on a wooden stretcher gives the framer a good starting point. The battening of a canvas gives the best chance to explore the making of mitre corners and to see the effect the crisp, straight line has on the rather rounded section of the stretcher.

A batten is simply a long, thin, flat piece of wood fixed like a thin frame to the edge of a canvas. This is a popular method often used by students, for when costs have to be kept in check, it both improves the appearance of a painting and gives some protection to rather vulnerable canvas, easily dented when stacked in studios and galleries. The battening therefore should stand proud of the face of the canvas by 5 mm to 10 mm (¼ in. to ⅛ in.), enough to give a projecting protective edge. Of course if the painting is going to be hung immediately, then this precautionary element need not be considered, but all the same the slight projection gives a better appearance. It also helps to conceal any irregularity at the side of the canvas.

Canvas has to be tucked and folded and tacked in place, and with thick canvas this can produce a surprising bulge, and because the battening will touch this, there inevitably will be a slight gap elsewhere. The projection of the battening beyond the face of the canvas will help to minimise the amount that is seen.

Battening 5 mm (¼ in.) wide by 25 mm (1 in.) deep should probably serve well. Both hard and soft wood can be used. Cutting soft wood is easier and any warpage is less violent, and panel pins are not so likely to split it, but knots in soft wood frequently drop right out of such a small, thin section. On the other hand hard wood will cut cleanly, keep its edges and probably be free of large knots, though splits can be more serious.

Buying wood for framing can be alarming. The little picture suddenly seems to grow as one calculates the length to buy. For instance 600 mm (24 in.) doesn't seem that large until it is multiplied by the four sides, then because of mitring there is some loss, so it would take about 2800 mm (9 ft). Do not have the salesman cut it into pieces but be careful how you shop with bits of material like this — it is soon possible to get into slapstick situations!

Strange, too, how cars and rooms shrink when wielding lengths of wood and framing. This will be the moment when comments about work area planning come to mean something. For the artist/craftsman a mitre box and a vice permanently fixed to a table can be a considerable nuisance when involved with other work, and certainly this is the case in the improvised work area. It is likely then that for a batch of frame

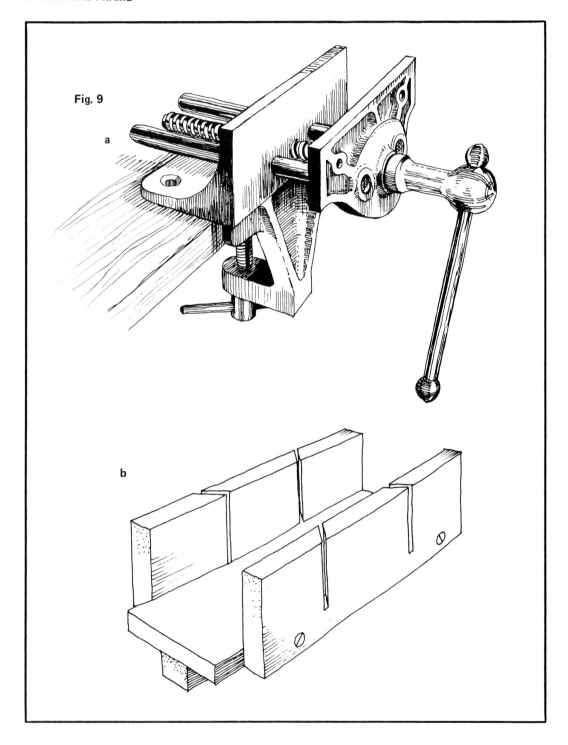

Fig. 9

a

b

making the vice will be fixed especially. I can predict that the first chosen position of vice on table and table in the room will mean that the newly bought wood will not fit the length between wall and mitre box. The trick here is to sight the line of the material being cut to pass through a doorway or window. Later with shorter pieces there will be no trouble. It will help the gaining of confidence and experience if with some of the first attempts at battening lengths of wood are cut off with a normal straight cut allowing more than enough for the mitre to be re-cut later. There will of course be some wood wasted as a result but it will probably make for a simpler beginning and a successful result.

With the left hand (each hand position will be reversed for those left-handed) hold the wood battening firmly against the far inside of the mitre box and the saw will then travel diagonally across to the right in the guiding slots provided. The cut should always be made 5 mm (¼ in.) from the end of the batten, making certain that a full angle is achieved. Trying to make the cut coincide with the end of the wood is likely to fail, so waste a little bit and get it right. Make the first cut.

Place the piece of battening on the table and stand the painting on it. Make an identifying mark on both the batten and the back of the stretcher. Mark the other three sides of the stretcher as well at this moment for later reference. By eye line up the inside corner of the mitre with the vertical side of the stretcher/painting. A straight edge or ruler placed vertically on the side will help the lining up, and will reveal the variations of canvas thickness I mentioned earlier, so consider it carefully.

When you are satisfied with that corner make a pencil mark at the other end where the surplus length will be sticking out — the pencil mark itself will have a width and so will the saw cut, so some thought, and no doubt some trial and error will have to be made to gain the particular

experience with your own marks, and saws, to enable the piece of wood to be cut ultimately exactly the right length. Then place the battening back in the mitre box with the freshly-cut end sticking out to the left; check that the cut you are about to make will be at the opposite angle to the first. Do not change the direction of the saw in the box, it will always be simplest to hold and make your cuts if it travels diagonally to the right. This also means that the outside edge of batten (or frame) will always lie against the far wall of the mitre box. Try the batten against the picture and check both ends.

Fig. 9a: A metal vice suitable for the frame maker.
Fig. 9b: A simple wooden mitre box having a 'U' section. Note the guiding slots and the block on the base for clamping in a vice.
Below: First mitre cut.

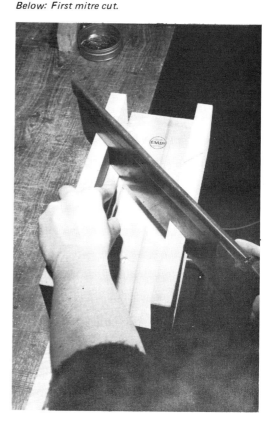

Now it is no fault of the frame maker if the painting being worked on is not quite rectangular. Of course he or she might be the painter as well — nevertheless by the very nature of stretchers and their adjustable corners it is quite likely that opposite sides will not be quite the same length. If they are, cut the second side to make a pair exactly the same size as the first and mark it for identification. If they are not the same, the first end should be cut and the second marked against the painting and cut exactly to its dimension. The second paired sides 3 and 4 should be treated in the same sequence.

Having made all the saw cuts it is tempting to sandpaper away any whiskers of wood. Don't! The corners will be rounded if you do and the crispness spoilt. The whiskers will also help to bed into one another and mask the joint. Any cleaning up should wait until the battening is on the picture, and just about the last refinement for the corner. The wood usually used for

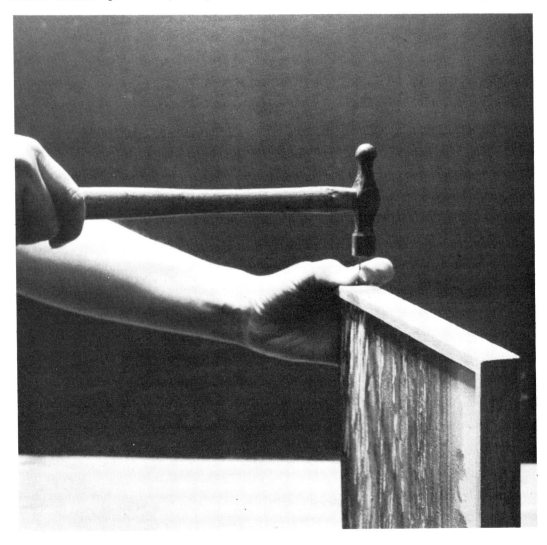

battening will have such a thin section that joining corners with glue and panel pins will hardly be practical or even necessary. It is at this stage that battening should be painted, before assembly. If no colouring is to be used on the batten, get your hammer and pins within reach of your right hand. Place the painting on the table, standing it on edge, take one appropriate batten, identified by the mark, and lay it along the top edge. Line up the back of the batten with the back of the picture. At the same time the ends must be aligned. Double and triple check.

When you are happy with the position, using the first finger of your left hand to line up the back of the batten with the back of the stretcher, hammer in one moulding pin about 25 mm (1 in.) from one end, then one similarly positioned at the other end, and at 150 mm (6 in.) intervals along its length. 20 mm (¾ in.) pins should be about the size, but it is near the corner that most strength is needed, and longer pins could be used there.

Place the canvas on a spacing block of wood to raise the jutting mitre from the table surface. Locate the second side. If the canvas in this position is too high for comfortable work, place the spacing block on a lower surface, such as a stool, and replace the canvas, on edge, on the block, and with the second side in place drive in the pins. Continue working your way round adding the third and fourth sides.

With a piece of medium fine sandpaper wrapped round a flat block of wood, sand the face of the battening at the corner, and on the outside at the corner. But never try to round the corner, it will spoil the crispness.

Left: Pinning the battening on the second side of the painting.
Below: Carefully sand the face of the battening at the corner. Do not round the corner.

You may know of local shops which stock a simple wooden frame section. Work out the total length of wood you will need; allow for slightly damaged ends on long lengths and for the extra you will need for cutting the mitres on your frame.

For the beginner or where space is limited and when there is some length to spare, cut the wood into four basic pieces with a normal right angled cut. Each piece is going to have two mitred ends. For example on a frame which has a thickness of 50 mm (2 in.), allow 60 mm (2½ in.) for the mitre x two in addition to the length of your picture edge. The procedure is the same for framing a canvas or a mounted work, except that canvas (as with battening) produces more lumps and bumps and the exact size is less easy to judge. Selecting a mounted work use just the backing card — it must be exactly the same size — and it will save the actual drawing from possible finger marks. Mark on the back of each piece of wood A and B respectively for the two shorter sides, and C and D for the longer. Place A in the mitre box, its back to the far wall of the box and the frame's face upwards. Cut the right hand mitre. Remove A from the box and lay the card in the rabbet 2 mm ($\frac{1}{16}$ in.) from the freshly cut mitre. Mark the other end on the wood and make a little reminder line showing which way the mitre will travel. Place A back in the box but back uppermost. Cut the second mitre. (It is very easy to be interrupted and to pick up a marked length of wood with a single dot and to proceed to cut it the wrong way!). Piece A is now complete. Do not sandpaper it. Select B which will be the opposite piece of the frame. Cut the first mitre as for A, then place A and B outside edge to outside edge, lining up the two cut mitres to make a sort of ship's bow. Mark on the back of B the exact point where the mitre of A ends. Place B back in the mitre box, back uppermost, and cut B's second mitre. The second two sides are cut in the same manner.

Below left: Marking the frames as illustrated will avoid confusion.
Below: Mark the mitre length with mounting card.
Right: Pairing two lengths for the second cut.

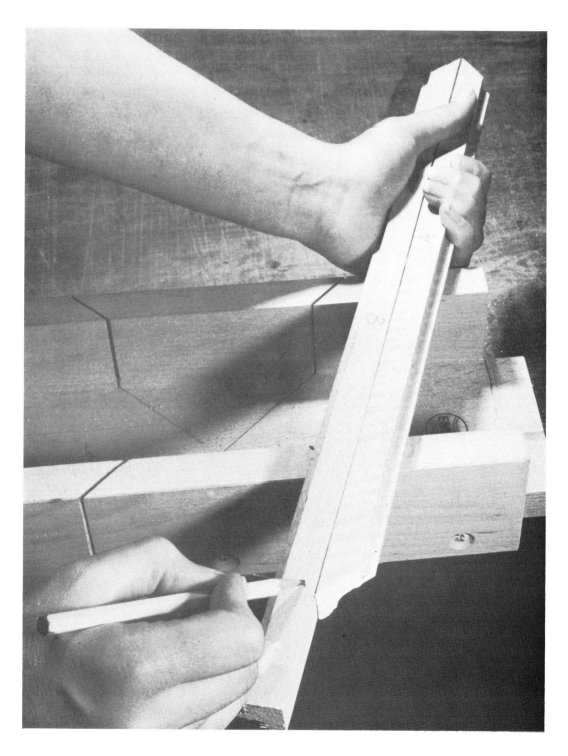

When cutting framing with the back upwards, the left hand must hold it firmly against the far side of the box. All cuts should just leave the mark on the wood for the frame — not the off-cut. It is the side you can see and will be simple enough when you are used to your saw and can judge the width of the cut it makes.

You should now have four pieces of framing. Two for the shorter sides A, B, and two for the longer C, D. An accurate square frame will only need the first side to be cut. With the care just described sides B, C and D will be cut taking A as the standard. This method of measuring one side against its partner, ensures that the finished frame is itself rectangular, even if the mount or canvas may be slightly out of true. The tolerance in the rabbet will take account of any variation. It is worth making a frame for a canvan bigger by 3 mm (1/8 in.) on each side — the position of the canvas can be then fixed by little packing pieces of card wedged in on each side. Remember a canvas may need tightening by knocking in wedges — see Chapter 7. This will make the whole picture slightly bigger and no frame will like having too big a picture crammed in to it. One corner is bound to break and there will be a nasty gap in the mitre. So with all these warnings — now the fixing of the four together.

Above: Holding the frame section in the vice, hammer in the pins.
Right: A frame side with the top ready.

If the picture is of a vertical shape, select the two shortest pieces, A and B. It is into these pieces the corner moulding pins will be driven. If the picture is of a horizontal shape, then select the two longer pieces. The reason is that two pins in each corner will be enough for most small frames if glue is used as well. This makes for a neater appearance from the side, with no pin heads to be seen. One rarely sees the top or bottom of a frame so this is where to put the pins.

Using only enough pressure to hold your frame without damaging its surface or denting it, place it in your vice (the wooden face pieces are valuable here). Drive in two pins so that their points just protrude mid way along the freshly cut mitre corner. Their length should be about two-thirds the width of the frame.

Move the frame in the vice to the other end for firm support and hammer in the other two pins. Similarly locate the pins in the other side (B). It does rather depend on the section of the frame you are using, but generally it will be found that to grip the frame between the outside edge and the edge of the rabbet will be the most satisfactory.

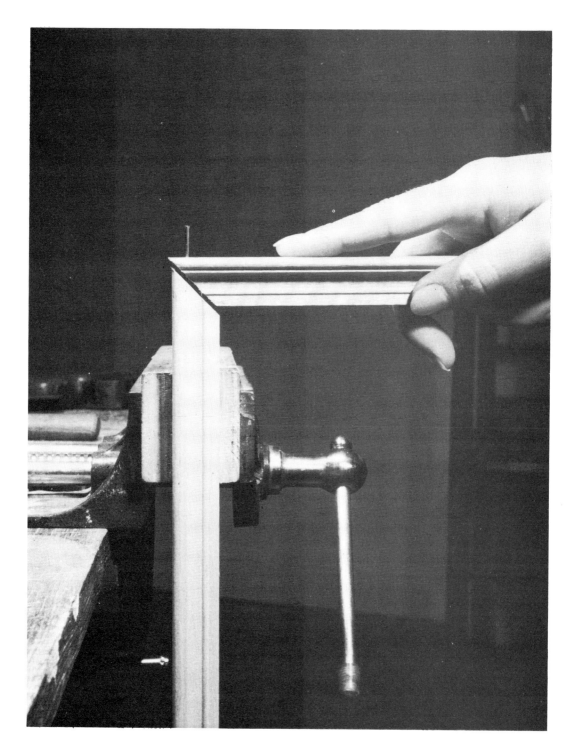

Place side D vertically in the vice, protruding about 50 mm (2 in.) above it. Stand to the right of the vice and work to your left. (You will be looking at the back of piece D sticking up in the vice.) With your hammer to hand, put a small quantity of wood glue on to the mitre surfaces. Then locate piece A on to D, slightly higher on the slope than a perfect match should be. There is a little knack in judging quite how much, but the reason is that as you hit the pin, there is a tendency for piece A to slide downwards. If you do not start high enough, by the time you have hammered home the pins you will find that piece A has slid down past a perfect match, and do what you will you cannot get it back! The best way is to start 5 mm (¼ in.) high, and still have a fraction to go when the pins are completely in. Then with a sharp tap of the hammer, move piece A down the last fraction. There is a good feeling inside when you get it just right! If you think you may dent the edge of the frame doing this, a block of wood interspaced will save damage. Slacken the vice.

Hold both sides of the L piece now assembled and lay it flat on the table. Repeat exactly with piece C in the vice and B being located on top. The two L pieces now have to be brought together with a little more support. C is held in the vice with B attached, but without support from below it will sag. So with a pile of books, possibly topped off with some magazines or pieces of mounting card, just take the weight of the end of B, while the other end of C is about 50 mm (2 in.) above the vice. Put a small amount of glue on to the surface of the mitre and locate the second L shape, A, D, and line up the back of the frame, but high in position. Drive home the pins and tap into the exact position for the mitre. With one hand holding the frame at its remaining unjoined corner, slacken off the vice and carefully turn the frame round and replace it in the vice to complete the final corner. A little glue into the joint, then the location, drive in the pins, a final tap and the frame is complete. Clean off any messy glue.

Synthetic wood glues can be removed with a water-dampened rag — they look white when applied but dry colourless. If you can bear to do so, let the frame lie quietly overnight for the glue to dry. If you do try it on your picture, do not get glue onto your mount. Do then leave it for the glue to dry. While this is happening you can measure for and obtain your piece of picture glass, generally of 18 oz weight. Allow it to be 3 mm (⅛ in.) smaller than the rabbet size. For cutting glass yourself see Chapter 6.

Though the wood can be left as it is with merely some white wax furniture polish to seal the surface, the possibilities for the colours of your frame are endless. You must consider the picture, the mount, the wall colour and the whole environment. The classic treatment is white, but light coloured frames can look very handsome with a dark mount. Use emulsion paint — it dries to a good even surface very quickly and white emulsion can be altered with any other water thinned paint — poster colour is particularly useful. The use of acrylic and polymer artists' paint is also excellent. Trials for colours can be made using off cuts, which as the collection grows can be a very useful reference. If the moulding is to have two colours, paint the paler all over first. Give a second coat and allow to dry. Then the darker, second colour

will easily cover in one application. Where you require a colour change, I suggest that you do so between any moulding shapes. Let the change of shape or direction be the point of change in colour or texture. Some beautiful soft effects can be obtained by rubbing a very thin smear of the second colour on to the first. If you don't like the effect, a rag with hot water will soon remove the paint. Another priming coat will remove any last trace.

Wood when varnished will tend to turn a much deeper and harsher colour. However some synthetic varnishes may satisfactorily seal the surface without changing the colour or adding too high a shine.

Gold or silver paint never really looks gold or indeed silver — they look like gold paint or silver paint and some have a granular texture which is very noticeable when used over the total area of the frame. But they are excellent for repairs and for lines or edges. Although excellent gold leaf framing is available from professional framers, the ancient and delicate craft of gilding is explained in connection with the repairing of old frames in Chapter 6.

Now though everything may have gone according to plan, when you come to fit the frame on your picture, there may be a moment when for all the calculations it does not fit. Try turning it round for this may just solve the problem. If not, don't despair.

If the mount is now slightly too large, with your cutting knife pare off a sliver on two sides (removing a little off one side will make the mount lopsided). Most faults will be found to be a wobble or bulge in the cutting of the card, or a dribble of dry glue.

If glass is the trouble or if the picture is on a stretcher, then you will have to enlarge the rabbet of the frame by hand. Any trouble will only be slight — a bump on the glass — and a sharp blade in your knife with the frame face down on your working table and all will be well.

Far left: The vice with the wooden block used to hold the frame steady.
Left: Hammering in the backing pins.

But it is a nuisance nonetheless when this happens and should give you experience to allow a little more when measuring next time.

Having too much clearance itself can bring difficulties — but mount, glass or stretcher can be easily positioned by pieces of mounting card used as packing. You might think that it does not matter if a mount is a little smaller than the frame, but if the opening has been cut with an equal border all round, the fact that it drops to the bottom of the frame will mean seeing more mount at the top and less at the bottom. This is never comfortable, so slide in packing to bring the mount to the correct height.

Small moulding pins 20 mm (¾ in.) long should be used to hold the picture in place. To do this lay the picture in its frame face down on the table, using newspaper or material to prevent scratching. Clamp a piece of wood with your vice or two metal clamps on the edge of the table. With the frame pressing against the block of wood, hammer in the pins towards yourself, sliding the hammer head on the backing card. Trying to do this hammering in mid air can well break the corners of the frame — even the glass.

If you have some masking tape — broad sticky paper tape — cover the joint between the frame and the backing card. Mitre the corners of the masking tape for neatness.

Once one has grasped the sequence and judgements important to the success of making a frame, it becomes a natural development to make up ones own sections.

A visit to your wood supplier — probably a shop selling a range of wood for domestic purposes, kitchen cabinets, pelmets, etc, will probably provide some small sectioned wood suitable for your framing use. Calculations become complex when invention starts, for what you imagine is suitable may in practice look uncomfortable. Thickness will be deceptive. If possible buy any odd short lengths and experiment at home. Start with a piece 100 mm (4 in.) wide x 7 mm (¼ in.) and on to this add other sections. The frame may well be heavy and could become quite expensive, but it can look very good and if you keep an eye open and tell your friends that you can use any bits they may no longer want, it is possible to collect material for practically no expense.

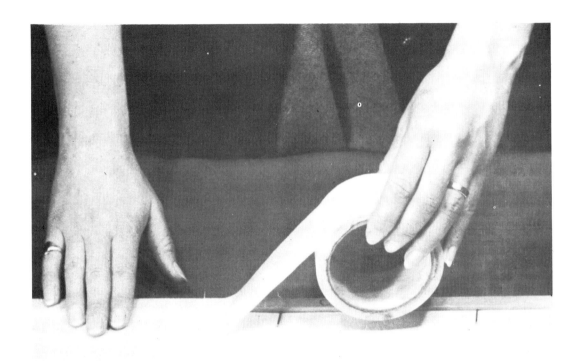

Left: Having secured the backing board, masking tape can be applied.
Right: The finished picture.
Bottom right: Made up frame sections.

If a frame is no wider than 25 mm (1 in.), all the moulding pieces should be fixed together, probably best glued, before the mitres are cut. But over this size there can be so much lost in the mitre that it would be a waste. A 100 mm (4 in.) wide frame can lose over 200 mm (8 in.) on the inside dimension. Therefore cut the main back piece and add all the extra mouldings, taking their measurement from the main back piece. Make up the frame only when all the cutting is complete. The most satisfactory sequence is likely to be to form the main background frame first, then to add the extra mouldings by gluing each in a complete circuit before moving on to the next moulding.

Aluminium is a different question. You can buy various lengths and sections and it is a simple task to polish it with wire wool, or kitchen scouring pads or scouring powder. Aluminium may well be most suitably used as a batten for a canvas, or it could be glued or screwed to the side of a frame. It will have to be cut with a special hacksaw blade. Small sections might be glued to the face of a frame to add a crisp, shiny line, but realise that as soon as your materials get more extensive, the price of your frame could quickly exceed that of a bought section.

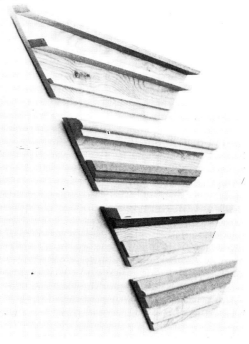

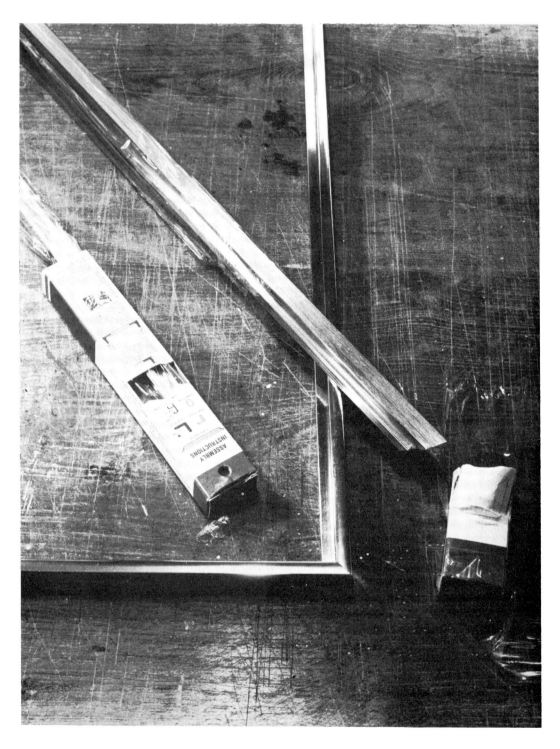

5 Frame variations

Further variations and combinations are possible using the bought frame kits which are available in a number of styles.

The aluminium sections are handsome and may be bought in 50 mm (2 in.) changes of length from about 200 mm (8 in.) to 1000 mm (40 in.). They are generally sold in a pack containing two sides, two packs making one frame. They are simple to assemble and are very, very strong at the corner joints; a valuable point for the exhibitor to consider where heavy handling may take place, and where works may want to be changed involving access to the picture. It is possible to dismantle these frames and swap sides, thus elements of two frames, one 305 mm x 610 mm (12 in. x 24 in.), the other 460 mm x 760 mm (18 in. x 30 in.) could be swapped to make a frame 305 mm x 460 mm (12 in. x 18 in.) and the other 610 mm x 760 mm (24 in. x 30 in.). Thus as long as the same brand is used infinite variations can be made and changes executed. With the addition of your own mounts the resulting picture will look very fine. Various frames for canvasses are also available in kit form.

I always think that objects in show cases in museums have a quality of looking precious. The single object behind glass in a shop window has a similar focus given to it. A canvas or drawing which wants to be totally seen, yet protected, can look very good in a glass fronted box. When the size has been calculated, cut the mitres of the box sides. Then assemble the sides, checking with a set square. Lay the rectangle on a piece of plywood or chipboard and mark on it the inside size of the box walls. This should fit snugly. If it is thick ply, screw

fixing can be made top and bottom (out of sight) directly through the side into the thickness of the plywood. If you are in doubt, edge the plywood at the back with a 5 mm (¼ in.) square section of wood and screw into this. Take account of the loss in depth on the inside of the box. The picture will be fixed to the plywood back which can be removed, so the glass can be made a fixed item. Cut a piece to lie half across the side walls and with a very thin piece of wood, just thicker than the glass, mitred at the corners, complete the surface to the outside edge of the wall. In place of wood a good substitute is thick mounting card or an aluminium strip. This is then covered by a thin batten of wood, again mitred at the corners, which will then trap the glass. The width of this batten should be equal or slightly wider than the width of the wall of the box. The strip at the side of the glass should be glued to the wall, the glass laid in the rabbet created and the top batten glued on top.

If the strip is metal it can be drilled first and the top batten fixed with the finest moulding pins, possibly brass. Beware of wood fillers with a spirit base. If the wood is subsequently varnished they can seal the surface where they were wiped over and cause a change in absorbency and thus a colour change, which looks horrid.

This box can be made in a variety of ways, and I realise that carpenters would happily rabbet the top edge of the wall — however the effect would be little changed.

A very old canvas, or a painting on a wood panel, possibly a damaged painting that would produce problems for normal frames and protection, could look very well in a box of this type. To place a canvas in such a box, simply stick two blocks of wood and the stretcher will hang on the top of them. Screws through the backing plywood might fix a less precious painting. Nylon-hooked tape which dressmakers use could also provide the solution.

Top left: *Detail of box corner.*
Bottom left: *Detail of the back of the box.*
Fig. 10: Cross section of box showing alternative fixing.
Below: *Box with facing tops.*

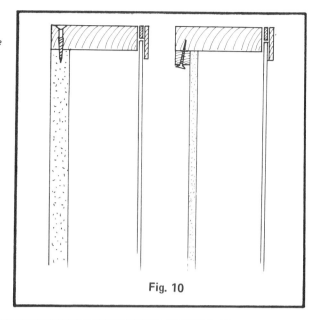

Fig. 10

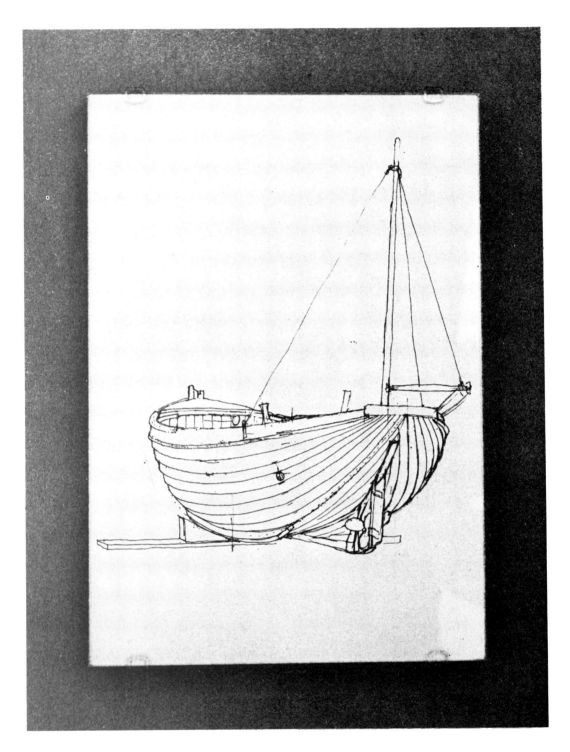

With some styles of interior design there is an emphasis on function and clearance of structure. A support for a drawing which virtually has no frame can look crisp and clean. The basis is a backing board of either plywood or chipboard, about 20 mm (¾ in.) thick. This can be cut to size more easily if it is clamped by the vice to the table top. A sheet of glass is cut to exactly the same size, but the sharp edges should be bevelled if possible. This you can do by carefully smoothing the sharp edge with a coarse emery paper or a fine sharpening stone. The glass is fixed with little metal or plastic L shaped clips which screw into the side of the backing board. This sort of frame is good for work on paper where no mount is needed, or where a paper mount is used — see page 19. It is a useful frame for a student for the work can be quickly changed. The screws fixing the clips will have to be repositioned if the thickness of the mounting material is altered. It is not a very safe method of framing for work which has to be transported, for the glass is easily broken. A less vulnerable version can be made which has a small batten of wood added round the outside edge of the board to act as a sort of buffer. At home this measure would be unnecessary.

A clear acetate such as perspex may be incorporated in some of the frames I have mentioned, but it does scratch easily, even in dusting, and it is not a cheap material. It does however have the advantage for the worker at home of being simple to cut and it is possible with perspex glue to stick it together so that variations on the box idea could be employed. A box lid of perspex could be mounted over a solid backing piece but there does come a moment when one really leaves the world of the frame maker and becomes the display maker. Again I would say that whatever is done, it is the object which should claim the attention, and the materials of the frame should not detract from that.

Left: The 'no frame' frame.
Above right: Fixing the clips.

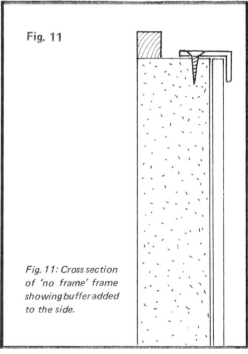

Fig. 11

Fig. 11: Cross section of 'no frame' frame showing buffer added to the side.

6 Old frames

Do nothing to an old frame until you are certain that it has no antique value. Your nearest antique furniture shop will guide you, or ask their advice as to whom you can consult. If the frame is in need of treatment, the following methods are quite possible.

Gold frames — that is frames covered with a white plaster-like ground called gesso, then a layer of red bole, and finally gold leaf on top — should never be washed or wiped or rubbed harshly. You will quickly remove the gold leaf and the red bole will be exposed. Rubbing further will then lay bare the white ground.

After a general clean up with white spirit — excellent because it does not dissolve water base-glue and does not leave any sticky deposit — replace any moulding with car body filler; there is a soft type which is easily cut and sanded even when dry. A complicated piece could be cast with the use of re-useable rubber mould material, particularly useful where a repeat pattern is involved.

At this stage one has the choice of the simple finish using gold paint, or the more complex process of using gold leaf. If you choose paint, match the gold to the nearest pot of gold paint you are able to buy — there are a number of

Right: Prior to restoring an old frame it is essential to clean it using white spirit.

shades — but only paint your repairs and spot any chips. Proprietary brands of gold preparations are available for touching up.

If the frame is a particularly fine one, and is in a relatively good state but has a few pieces of moulding broken, then it could well be worthwhile, after the addition of filler and shaping the

required parts, to continue the gilder's process to enable you to relay gold leaf. It will be expensive. A book of gold leaf containing 25 sheets about 80 mm (3¼ in.) square will most probably cost more than many simple bought frames, but the quality of the repaired frame will be restored.

The gilder's craft is very ancient and like many other crafts is simple in many ways, yet full of deft skills acquired only with practice and the observation of others doing it. However, though the beginner may be clumsy when compared to the expert, he can still succeed to the degree required. You will need a gilder's cushion, a gilder's knife and a gilder's tip. The gilder's cushion or board 150 mm x 200 mm (6 in. x 8 in.) is made from a piece of card covered on the top side with a thin pad of cotton wool and itself covered by a soft piece of calf leather — suede side up. A finger loop for holding is made at the back.

Having made the basic shape of the repair one needs to coat this with a very, very smooth coating — this is called a gesso ground. Much has been written on this subject and it makes fascinating reading. However I shall describe a process which I hope will not offend professional gilders, but which is simple to follow, and what is important for the amateur — it works! This first method is called water gilding.

Rabbit skin glue, by the sheet or in granulated form, should be soaked in water overnight. It will take up its own weight of water and swell to jelly like lumps.

A double boiler — a container which sits in a larger second container holding water is brought to a state where the heating water in the lower container is just on boiling. The glue is then diluted by about 15 parts water to one of glue — this is very approximate. Warm water can be used which will speed up the process of melting the little lumps. The test for the glue is that

Left: Preparation of gesso ground.
Right: Gold leaf tools. From top to bottom: Gilder's cushion, gold leaf book, agate burnisher, gilder's knife, gilder's tip and red bole.

it should just stick the finger and thumb together when wetted with the glue and blown dry. Of course the skin will not completely stick, but the adhesion will be felt. The look of the glue when cool and set will be like a table jelly. This thin glue is the medium and should be kept warm.

On a piece of glass or other flat surface, pour a small pile of whiting — chalk. With a palette knife mix a little glue into the powder until a smooth cream results. If this thickens, it can be transferred to a saucer and placed over the steaming water in the boiler to make it more liquid again. This preparation is laid on to the necessary parts of the frame with a soft brush and allowed to dry. This coating can be sanded with very, very fine sandpaper and the process repeated until the smoothest surface possible is obtained.

Red bole, a sort of red earth colour, is then put on a clean surface and with a little glue and palette knife, ground into a thin cream. This is painted over the dry white areas of the gesso and allowed to dry. The red bole is optional, but it adds a good underlying tonal quality.

Next a small jar of thin warm glue has about 20 per cent methylated spirit added to it. This should be put ready to hand with a soft sable brush close by.

The gilder's cushion is picked up. The tissue paper leaved book containing the gold leaf is carefully opened. One sheet of gold leaf is lifted with the gilder's knife and placed onto the cushion. It is straightened out with the help of the knife and then by drawing the knife gently across the surface, cut. Be generous enough with the piece you cut to more than cover the patch. Damp the area of bole to be covered with the glue/meths liquid. The gilder's tip — a broad flat brush made of card and hair — is then given a slight static charge by being drawn across the face or hair, and then touched onto

Right: Smoothing the gesso in a difficult hollow.

Far right: Red bole is painted on after the gesso has dried.

the piece of leaf. It will adhere enough to re-move it from the cushion, and then lay the leaf onto the frame.

Lightly press the leaf down with a piece of cotton wool. Continue laying leaf on all the areas and leave the frame to dry overnight. Next day lightly brush away unstuck pieces of leaf and with an agate burnisher gently bring a smooth pressure to bear on the newly applied leaf and rub the burnisher backwards and forwards. The gold will obtain a high lustre.

The second method is called oil gilding. It re-quires the same smooth gesso surface and the red bole gives a good rich ground tone, although this again is optional. Next coat the areas which may be quite absorbent with shellac to seal them. The next stage is to apply Japan Gold Size

which can be obtained ready made in the bottle from Artist's Colourmen. It is a special mixture of copal varnish and dryers. This is applied to the areas and allowed to dry for one hour. It will then be just tacky enough to receive the gold leaf.

The shelac can be applied to paper or any other absorbent surface, and followed by the Japan Gold Size, followed by the leaf application. The limitation of the oil gilding is that the leaf can-not be burnished.

If the gold leaf is in a bad state and may even already be covered with gold paint, then it is quite possible to paint the whole or part of the frame. The most extreme treatment is to leave the frame out to the weather — or to soak it in water — and gradually the plaster will drop off. The resulting basic wood frame can then be given a scrub and a wax polish.

If the frame is covered in any form of ground or plaster, the ground material will chip and

Left: Lifting gold leaf.
Below: Gold leaf on the gilder's tip.
Below right: Smoothing with the agate burnisher.

fail to give a crisp, clean joint when re-cut. In some cases it may be very hard and will stand proud of the freshly cut mitred wood beneath. But re-mitring most small sectional frames presents no great problem. Check on the capacity of your mitre box — many old oil painting frames, even with their plaster mouldings removed, are quite wide and will not fit. If a frame is to be reduced in size, and the existing mitres are sound, consider cutting only two diagonally opposite corners. Rather like cutting a cake — a very thin slice is much more difficult than a good hunk. If you are trying to remove only 10 mm (⅜ in.) you may have to cut through nails. This will need a fine long hacksaw which will be guided by your mitre box slots. If more can be removed to provide you with a frame of your required size, cut the frame either side of one corner with a saw, and repeat these two cuts at the corner diagonally opposite. The two L shaped pieces can now be re-mitred, though the weight of the additional side attached may need an extra helping hand to take the weight while you concentrate on maintaining the position of the frame to cut the mitre. Easiest of all is to detach all corners and re-mitre and completely reassemble. The rejoining presents no special problem except that the

Left: Breaking the mitre on an old frame. Right: When re-finishing with gold paint, masking tape is useful and will give a clean straight line.

wood may be very hard and reject soft moulding pins. It is quite possible that splitting may occur so two fine holes drilled first will help a lot, though the points of the nails pushed through them should be used to guide any holes made in the other receiving half of the mitre.

If you are in doubt or troubles start, abandon nails altogether and with the use of clamps, or piles of heavy books or bricks, hold the frame in place with glue alone in the joint. Wood glues or impact glues are good (ie those that are applied to both surfaces and after a short

time the two surfaces can be brought together). Any useless holes can easily be filled with a wood or plastic filler and spotted with an appropriate spot of paint. Do not forget the staining power and filling quality of a wax shoe polish — forced well into the joint (this is where the whiskers left on cut wood can help) and the surplus rubbed off with a rag. Even coloured pencils are useful for toning in repairs. But do not get overconcerned about variations. It is the total effect which will be noticed, not the little blemish, when the frame is finally on the wall.

OLD FRAMES

Many older oil paintings were framed with exceedingly thick, heavy glass. Most oil paintings will look and be better off without this layer. But water colours and drawings will still require glazing. Old glass can become very brittle and since most people do not stock large pieces of glass, the most straightforward and economical solution is a visit to your local glass merchants. They will help you decide what weight/thickness you require. Do give them exact sizes — 2 mm ($\frac{1}{18}$ in.) less than the opening. Personally I do not like non-reflective glass — the slightly textured surface is often more obvious than the reflections. The whole quality of drawings, water colours and prints is the surface and the ability to actually see every finest mark and change. Any glass which limits this, to my mind clouds what you can see. If you do have a large sheet of glass and require a smaller piece

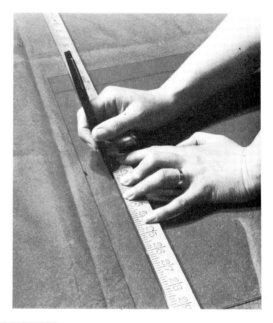

Above: Marking the glass before cutting. Left: Cutting the glass. Notice the position in which the cutting tool is held. Right: The glass is snapped along the cut line.

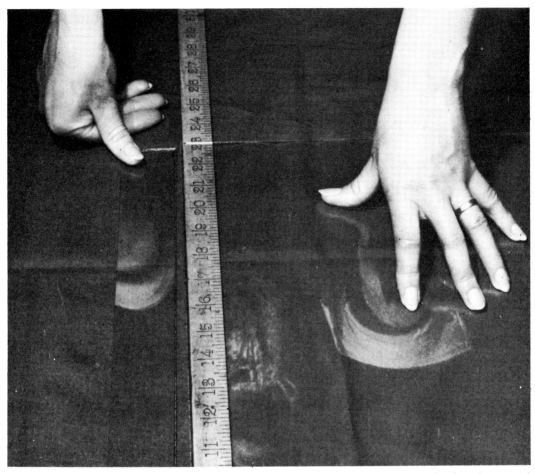

you will need a glass cutter, a straight edge, a T square or a set square, and a piece of felt or other material on which you can lay your glass. Mark out the size with care and decide which side of the line you are going to score. A special pencil for marking glass is useful, but a fibre tip pen will make a perfectly clear line, though it is instantly smudgeable. All lines must be taken right through from edge to edge of the sheet of glass. You cannot cut a corner out leaving an L piece over as you can with a sheet of mounting card.

With your straight edge as a guide, press the glass cutter firmly onto the glass surface. You will feel it bite into the glass and while you move the cutter you must maintain a downward pressure. Ensure you have incised the line right to the edges both at the start and finish. Slide your straight edge under the glass to the immediate left of the line and press the right hand side down — the glass should snap cleanly.

There is a knack, and though of course glass can cut, you must not be frightened of the material. A firmness of handling is required. However you may prefer to get an experienced man to provide your glass if you are in any doubt, but if you collect it, go prepared with material or corrugated cardboard for wrapping and a flat site to lay it out of harm's way when you bring it into the house.

7 Display

Cart before the horse — or horse before the cart? Do you have a wall and find a picture which looks well on it — or do you have a picture for which you have to find a happy wall? Impossible for me to answer. There are some basic points to consider and some basic do's and dont's but the ultimate choice is yours.

When you are considering the redecoration of a room or house, do not just think of walls and curtains. If you have pictures plan how the wall colours will show them to best advantage, and just thinking often is not enough. Ideas which remain in the mind can be disastrous when carried out. Samples of colours on a paint manufacturer's card look so completely different when seen over a large area. It is worth trying samples, even if you are confident. Buy the smallest tin of your wall colour and paint a piece of card or hardboard and prop it up in your room and live with it for some days — prop your pictures along side it and look at them at different times of the day. This sort of trying out — not just thinking it out — is most important. I have seen attractive little pictures looking very lost on a big expanse of wall. Do not be frightened by big pictures — the idea that you have to 'stand back from them' is not always true. Sometimes a large picture, about 1200 mm x 1500 mm (4 ft x 5 ft) can be hung in a small sitting room, but viewed from a neighbouring room as well through the open door. Much of the day doors are left open and one's own enjoyment should be continual. So don't rule out any sites in your house without experimenting.

Below: A small picture looking totally lost.

If you have more than one small picture, consider making a group close together on one
wall. Frame them in a similar style, or use
similar colours, or let them contrast with one
another — some quiet, some strong; some nar-
row, some wide.

Another fault I have noticed is that of hanging
pictures too high on a wall. Many can be
'looked into' with a great deal of pleasure, so
their centres should rarely be above eye level.
Perhaps some thought should be given to picture heights from a sitting position. There are
hazards of course. The pine chest has an added

Above: A group of pictures hung above a chest.
Right: A large painting viewed through a door.

importance with its oil painting hanging above —
fine that is until you open the lid to those for-
gotten treasures and bang the lid on the picture.

People referring to pictures they dislike, laugh
and talk of hanging them in the lavatory — but
why not have a print or a map there. Bath-
rooms and kitchens are rejected by some for
reasons of steam, or grease, but if non-precious
pictures, prints or magazine pages are framed,
they can have an attractive life and then should

*Below: A picture hung in a kitchen can look attractive
and change the character of the room.*
*Right: A group of nails and screws with plugs. On the
left of the group is a bolt with an expandable casing.*

any staining or marks occur, they, like the paint-work, can be replaced, and a pleasant job for the home frame maker.

Radiators and various forms of heating appliance can do harm for though the warmth itself may not harm a work, it is the dirt caught up in the upward current of air which will in time build up on picture surfaces — and this applies in the cleanest of houses. Here one would choose a glazed work, with a frame which could be easily wiped clean.

To hang a picture, one of the most valuable and simple aids is the masonry nail. This specially hardened, thickish nail can be bought in various lengths and with slow regular hits with a hammer, it can be driven into most brick walls. It should always bite into the brick, for the surface plaster covering will not take much load. man made types of compressed board covering wall will receive any sort of nail, preferably with a head; but wood coverings, like panelling,

are best drilled first — saving a possible split — and using a screw. Many houses will be built with the same materials throughout, so trials in one place will guide you elsewhere.

Now the job will be quite simple except in the case of a very hard wall when it may need a hole to be drilled with a drill using a masonry bit, and a special plug to fill the hole into which the screw is to go. An alternative, suitable for very heavy objects, is a bolt which screws into an expandable casing. The whole unit is pushed into the hole, of an exact matching size, and the screw is then carefully removed; the object or a metal hook is offered into place and the screw replaced. As the screw is tightened the casing in the wall expands and tightens in the hole.

I think it is important to choose the right handling of the wall first, as this will in some way dictate the fixings on the back of the picture.

Now the greatest number of pictures can be satisfactorily hung by screwing in two small eyes, about 80 mm (3 in.) from the top of the picture. Between these two points some thin 20 gauge, galvanised wire is stretched. The wire when taking the weight of the picture will pull upwards a little. It should be tensioned so as not to get nearer than about 40 mm (1½ in.) from the picture top. This 'wire to the top of the picture' distance can be marked on an odd piece of card. Find the middle of the top of the picture and mark it in some impermanent way. Then hold your picture up in its chosen position, make the tinest dot on the wall with a hard pencil, exactly at the centre top, and remove the picture. The distance marked on the card now indicates the distance which the nail must be placed below the mark on the wall. The masonry nail is then driven into the wall, slightly pointing downwards into the wall. Its head should be left about 10 mm (⅜in.) from

Below: A screw eye with attached wire.
Right: Marking the distance between the wire and frame top.
Bottom right: Marking the measurement on the wall.

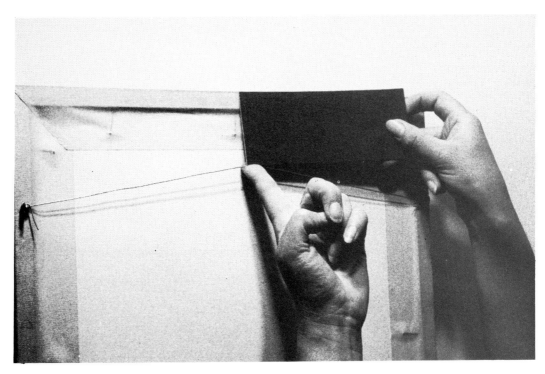

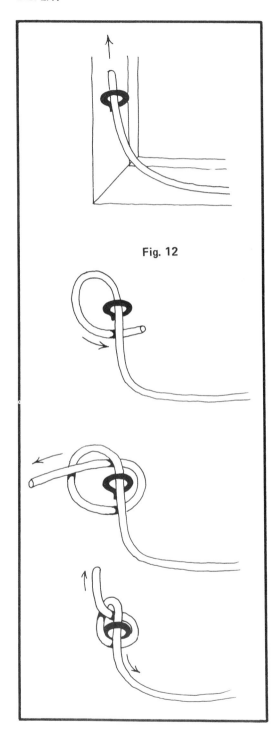

Fig. 12

the wall surface. The picture is then hooked onto the nail and adjusted to a horizontal position. The downward slope of the nail will carry the wire close to the wall and give the greatest strength. This basic method shows no sign of the fixing from the front of the picture. Do not use string instead of wire, for hanging. It will rot in time and your picture will fall. There is an exception to this — thick, smooth string is ideal for use in a temporary exhibition. The nails can be put in the wall quickly by judging heights, and the picture moved up or down by slipping the single twist in the string through the screw eye.

This basic method may have to include modifications to some very light frames — most likely in bought frames with attractive moulding or colour, but little 'twist' strength. This twist is caused by the pull of the wire across the back of the picture, and when the rabbet depth is great this levering action of the wire on the screw eye can distort the side members. This can be overcome by either hanging each side separately with a single wire going up virtually on to its own wall fixing or another method is to use a backing piece, such as hardboard, with a bar of wood glued to it, the screw eyes being screwed into the wood: or a backing which is of blockboard which can be screwed into directly.

Framers generally provide little screw eyes with a ring attached. I have never found these to be very satisfactory, for I do not like the sloppiness if wire is attached to the ring — or if a nail is put in the wall (hardened pins through a little brass hook can be bought for this purpose) the pin has to go into the wall awkwardly, near to sight at the edge of the picture and not easy to correct alignment. If you want to move the picture the mark on the wall is inevitably revealed, whereas a single nail has a better chance of never being revealed.

If the picture is heavy and the wall of questionable condition and/or if the picture is to lie absolutely flat against the wall, then a completely different method can be used — in fact using the system used for mirrors, ie mirror plates. These are made of brass or other metal and are of a stubby T shape. Two holes lie in the crosspiece which takes two fixing screws into the picture or object frame and will be countersunk on that side. The third hole lies in the rounded stem which takes the fixing into the wall, and is countersunk on the appropriately opposite side. When using these mirror plates, notice which side has the bevelled countersunk hole, taking the neck shape of the screw, and use accordingly. Two or four of these mirror plates will produce a very firm fixing. For minimum sight, place top and bottom of the frame. But when in place the part of the plate which is seen can be painted with a colour to match the wall; mat paint is best, it does not show ridges.

Fig. 12: A sequence showing the way that an exhibition knot should be tied.
Below: With a heavy picture the most effective way of securing it to a wall is with mirror plates usually made of brass
Below right: A canvas with protruding nail.

Two masonry nails spaced about 455 mm (18 in.) apart, on a well chosen level, will provide a perfectly adequate fixing for a canvas alone, or lightly battened, and has the added advantage to the painter that the work can be lifted off the nails standing out from the wall only 15 mm (½ in.), and replaced with another. And since stretchers are the same size (most painters will find an advantage in working with either a 45 mm or 50 mm [1¾ in. or 2 in.] standard) then even a painting with dimensions of 1200 mm (4 ft) could still be hung on the two nails, as long as they originally were placed on a central axis of the wall, allowing picture space at both sides. One warning though — since the stretcher is hanging on the nail, there is no protection between the nail head and the canvas, so the length of the protruding nails must be checked very carefully; if not they could easily puncture the canvas.

One has of course to weigh up the situation for oneself. As a painter, paintings and drawings in my house never seem to stay in one place for very long. So I choose to use secure but the most versatile fixings — allowing groups to be adjusted and added to, and as just described pictures replacing one another as they are removed from the easel.

Fig. 13

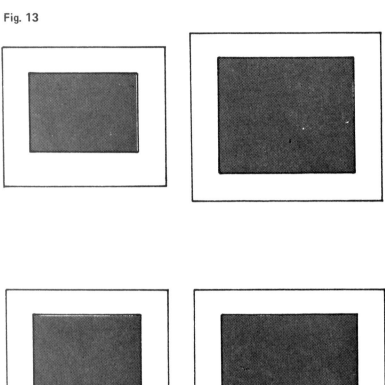

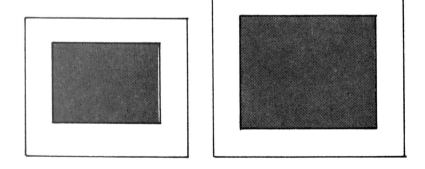

For those of you who enjoy making frames, what may seem permanent this year, may be given a new site next. On the other hand some pictures may have a permanent place, certainly until the next room redecoration, and for these situations it would be correct to use a very precise and permanent fixing designed only for the one picture.

Group hanging can at first glance look complicated, but not really if you work to one or two rules. The 'lane' system gives a unity to any group and has the added advantage that additions can be made to the group which does not require the earlier pictures being repositioned. Two pictures would hardly qualify as a group, but the 'lane' or gap between them is important if they are to have the feeling of two pictures together, and not just of two pictures hanging on the same wall. Of course it is a question of actual size and the lightness or darkness in appearnace of the pictures. A rough guide would be to space them the width of the mount apart, ie if a 100 mm (4 in.) mount is on the picture then the wall left between frame and frame, side by side, or one above the other, would be 100 mm (4 in.). If in doubt keep the frames closer rather than further away from one another. There is a sort of visual magnetic pull which will exist between the pictures — too close and they will disturb one another; too far away and they begin to look separate. If the picture is an oil, then the gap could well be the width of the frame or 100 mm (4 in.), whichever is the larger.

Clear an area on the floor and experiment. There are three possible side by side lining up methods for two pictures not quite the same size.

1   The middle line of each picture lining up with the other.
2   Tops lining up.
3   Bottoms lining up.

For two pictures near the same size, probably the best will be to line up middles, but if there is a considerable difference, say one-third bigger, then probably bottoms lining up will give the calmest relationship.

Three pictures of near the same size are best in a row with middles lining up, but if one is

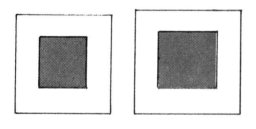

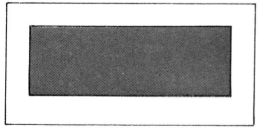

Fig. 13: Three ways of hanging two pictures side by side.
Fig. 14: One way of hanging three pictures.

Fig. 14

Fig. 15

larger, line up to tops or bottoms. If the three are made up by two small and the third about twice the size of the others, the two smaller can be placed above the larger. (A good rule here — pictures smaller or lighter in appearance should always be above another work). The lane between the two smaller will be the same as the lane between the two smaller and the larger.

With four pictures or more the lane method now becomes most useful. Whatever the variations of pictures it maintains an organised look, yet preserves the ability to put pictures anywhere within the system. Try out your 'four' arrangement on the floor. Choose the first, place number two by its left side with the 102 mm (4 in.) lane separating them. Place number three above two so that their right hand edges line up, and place number four a lane width away and with its left hand edge lining up with the left hand edge of picture number one. Of course you can try out changing the positions of pictures, but the principle remains the same, the cross lane maintaining the order.

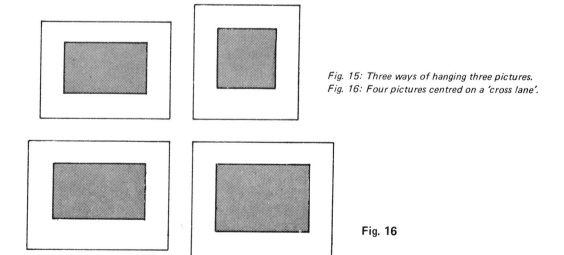

Fig. 15: Three ways of hanging three pictures.
Fig. 16: Four pictures centred on a 'cross lane'.

Fig. 16

81

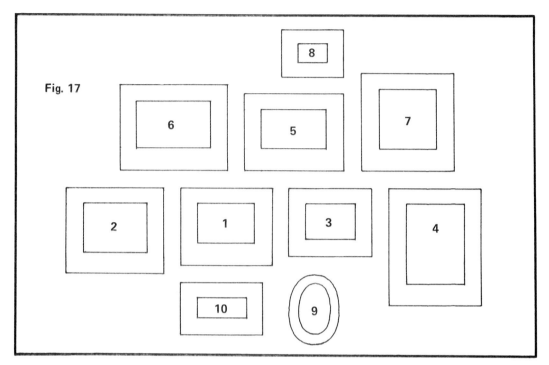

Fig. 17

For most domestic wall areas a basic two row system will be found convenient, but if the wall area upwards and downwards allows, it can grow. Start with your favourite and lay it on the ground. To its left lay a second picture, line up the tops; to the right a third, line up the tops; a fourth to the right again. Now work on the second row above the first and with picture number five place it partly above one and partly above three; then add six to the left and seven to the right. If there is room, eight, nine and ten could be added in the 'holes' above and below; but those above five, six and seven, must line up with one of the boundaries below them.

In figure 17 eight lines up with five (the lane to the right is maintained). Below nine lines up with the left of three, and ten lines up with the left of the favourite first. Those added into the holes should never be centred to those above, below, or left or right, but lined up one side or the other to maintain the lane on one side. If a circular or oval frame is part of the group, then line it up as if a rectangle were constructed, the boundary of which touched the oval, and it will obey the same rules.

There may be a room which demands a horizontal at the base of the group — for example where the wall surface changed from plaster to panelling. In this case line up the first row with bottoms in line. Build upwards, possibly maintaining one or two main lines vertically.

Groups on the wall of a staircase can be very pleasant. Frequently a difficult place to reach to hang one big painting, a collection of family photographs, animals, houses, can be a simple solution. Here the group can grow upwards and sideways by maintaining the lane and lining up at least one side each time. The group will look so much more attractive than the regular beat of one frame, one frame, one frame — reminding me of advertisements on the walls of Underground escalators.

Water colours can be adversely affected by

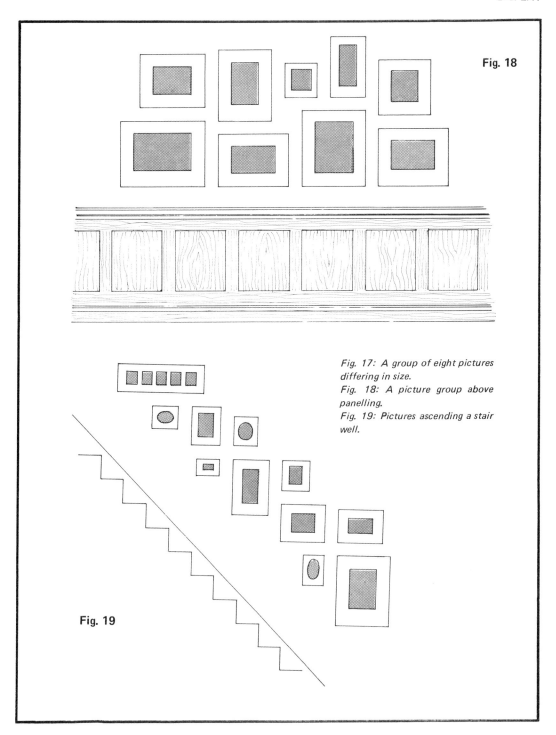

Fig. 18

Fig. 17: A group of eight pictures differing in size.
Fig. 18: A picture group above panelling.
Fig. 19: Pictures ascending a stair well.

Fig. 19

Left: A group of six pictures.
Right: A free standing spotlight can light pictures with ease, cheaply.

strong direct sunlight, so avoid positions where this can occur for prolonged periods. However it is when daylight fades that special thoughts should be given to illumination.

Lighting can affect the whole atmosphere of a room and all too often lighting pictures is not given enough importance. Purpose made picture lights are sometimes rather worrying for they can distract the eye from the actual picture.

Often a spot light is preferable. These can be very small and located on the ceiling or the ends of pelmets — free standing or standing on tables or chests, possibly partly hidden by flowers or other objects. These latter, pointing upwards, can light pictures with great ease and the minimum of installation and expense. Of course if you can plan in lighting when the house is being wired or re-wired, some of the

track systems might be employed. The track is a long metal slot which carries the electrical current. Lamps of the system are locked into the slot, their position being infinitely variable along the length of the track. A close look into shop windows will probably reveal a system of this type.

Some people do not like the rawness of spot lights, even if they are covered by a casing, in which case table lamps, hanging lamps and standard lamps can be carefully positioned so that they throw as good a light as possible on the pictures. Not always ideal to see the real quality of pictures, but pleasant for the atmosphere of the room.

Pictures need very little care once they are hung. Those with glass will need to have the glass cleaned, but take care not to rub the frame, for any surface can be removed over a period of time by abrasive rubbing. Use a dry, light cloth for frame dusting.

Room temperature should where possible be constant. Oil paintings are particularly vulnerable to temperature and humidity changes. Canvas can become floppy and wrinkles will appear. Do nothing to canvas if the reason for the changes is obvious and temporary. If however over a period of stable house and climatic conditions the slackness remains, take the picture down and lightly tap the corner wedges further in to expand the wooden stretcher slightly, which in turn will tighten the canvas. On no account over-tighten the canvas for old material could split.

A new painting needs no varnish — oil paint takes months to dry out fully and under normal conditions oil paint does not get dirty quickly. The lightest damp soft cloth will remove any film of dirt.

If the painting dries with an uneven surface, glossy in some places, mat in others, due to variations in the oil content of the paint, a thin coat of synthetic varnish produced by a reputable artists' material manufacturer should be applied to the whole surface. Some old varnishes turned yellow, and what was worse, could not be removed. Modern varnishes can be removed simply with white spirit, double rectified paraffin (sometimes called turpentine substitute). To varnish the picture remove it from its frame. However I must emphasise that though some art work is quite robust and with care and some commonsense treatment, will not be harmed, much could be damaged irrevocably by harsh cleaning or handling. If you have any pictures about which you know no definite facts, seek specialist advice first. The sort of people to ask will vary with the type of work but most museums and public art galleries have experienced staff, and allocate certain times for dealing with such enquiries. It is not always possible to depend on the advice a shop assistant will give you. They may be experienced in selling attractive frames, but not all by any means are experienced in identifying work!

But once you know that yours is not an original Rembrandt etching, then you can clear your table, put on your apron and start framing.

Top left: A sloppy canvas.
Top right: To tighten the canvas lightly tap the wedges.
Left: A painting properly stretched, framed and hung.

GLOSSARY

The descriptions relate to the usefulness to the frame maker

ADVICE Some museums and galleries offer expert advice on identifying works of art at special times as a service to the public. Check with the administration departments first

BATTEN A thin flat strip round the edge of a painting — generally made of wood

BIT A metal rod spirally grooved and with a cutting tip. A great range of sizes

BOLE An earth pigment containing red iron oxide which when mixed with water glue is used to give a ground colour prior to applying gold leaf

BRADAWL A metal point with a handle for making an introductory hole in wood

CANVAS Linen canvas is the best artist material. Cotton and jute are less satisfactory

CHALK Prepared Calcium Carbonate. Natural chalk is called *whiting*. Obtainable from chemists in powder form. Other fine white pigment can be added to chalk to improve covering power, eg titanium dioxide

DRILL The most useful hand operated drill is the wheel brace, having a side wheel geared to the turning head. The actual cutting piece is called a *bit*

DRY MOUNTING PAPER A thin paper coated on both sides with a heat softened glue. Used by photographers for mounting photographs onto card. A propreitary brand of glue in a pressurised container is available which performs a similar function

EMULSION PAINT A synthetic paint which though thinnable by water, on drying is not dissolved by it. Various types of synthetic resin are used which may be found in their description. They are excellent and clean to use

ETCHING Made by etching with acid the lines and textures of the picture into a metal plate. Ink for printing the picture is introduced into the lines and the surface wiped clean. Dampened paper is used and the pressure of the printing press squeezes the two together The shape of the metal plate is clearly seen beyond the boundary of the picture

GOUACHE PAINTING A painting using pigment (also known as *poster colour*) carried in water based glue and applied in opaque areas with the use of white pigment to control the final tones obtained

GILDER'S CUSHION A card or board padded with a thin layer of cotton wool and covered with soft leather, suede side up. A loop at the back for holding

GILDER'S KNIFE A broad steel knife with a crisp angled end. An old bread knife of large proportion can serve well, or a modified large palette knife or spatula

GILDER'S TIP A very broad flat brush with the hairs set in a flat card handle

GLASS Glass suitable for pictures has a thickness of about 2 mm ($\frac{3}{32}$in.) Non-reflective glass — a finely dimpled surfaced glass which while not changing the view of the picture a great deal, limits reflections

GLASS CUTTER A special tool, frequently made with a rotatable head giving several replacement cutting wheels

GOLD LEAF Incredibly thin sheets of gold sold in books, tissue paper separating the sheets numbering about 25. Variations of colour are obtainable depending on the range from 16 carat to 23.5 carat Silver leaf is also available

GLUE A great variety available — three types useful to the framer
Rubber based type suitable for paper to paper, material to card
Wood working — synthetic — looks white when fresh, colourless when dry
Impact — applied to both surfaces to be joined and when part dry makes an instant fix when the two surfaces are brought together
Rabbit skin — bought by the sheet or granulated. A water dissolved glue traditionally used by the artist craftsman. It has a short life when wet, quickly going bad. If burnt in heating it will lose its adhesive quality. Use a double boiler to prevent this

GROUND An underlying coating on a painting or frame. Essential in making adhesion between the painting and canvas, or gold leaf and wood

HAMMER A cross-pein 100 gm (3½ oz) is the most useful. The engineer's version called the ball-pein has a domed head one side instead of a thin flat head found on one side of the cross-pein. Care with the cross-pein though — its thin flat head can make nasty dents if misused

JAPAN GOLD SIZE A proprietory mixture of copal varnish and dryers. Used for gilding

KNIFE An all purpose craft knife with a good large handle to grip. Replaceable blades essential. Some small craft knives for model making are too fragile for mount cutting

LITHOGRAPHY	Invented about 1796 by Senefelder, it has become with modern technology one of the most versatile of printing processes. In its original form it uses limestone blocks, ground smooth, and a greasy drawing from which by a process of replacement the print is taken while the stone remains damp; the separation of image and non-printing areas depending upon the antipathy of oil and water
MASONRY BIT	See Tungsten bit
MASONRY BOLT	A bolt which, on being tightened, expands part of its casing to tightly fit the hole into which it is placed
MIRROR PLATE	A metal stubby T shaped plate screwed to an object leaving part to be screwed to a wall
MITRE	Joint of two pieces of wood at an angle of 90° with the line of the junction bisecting this angle
MITRE BOX	A guide made of wood or metal which guides a saw for cutting mitres
MOUNT	A surround to a picture — usually made of stiff card
NAILS	Nails as such are not commonly used — see Pins
OIL PAINTING	A painting using pigment carried in a mixture of oils, capable of being used transparently or opaquely. Because the oils change their chemical state by combining with oxygen they dry from the outside inwards. The final drying time can be many months
PENCILS	A medium grade — 2B. Hard grades damage the surface of cards. Very soft grades lose their precise point
PINS	Panel pins/moulding pins — a thin round nail with a very small head
PLIERS	Metal pincers having flat or pointed jaws and with a wire cutting notch
PRINT	A broad term but concerned with a process in which the artist prepares the picture personally and makes identical or near identical prints by the process concerned. Frequently an edition will be of a stated number, and each print numbered. Artists' proofs describing works made prior to the edition proper. Many commercial processes have been added to the range possible but these tend to be directed to mass production as opposed to the individual attention the artist/print maker can give
PUTTY	Proprietory brands of adhesive putty for temporarily fixing paper to another surface. A quantity the size of a match head is enough to stop a picture slipping under glass

RABBET	The hollow step in the back of a frame section to take the picture
RUBBERS	A medium grade. Hard grade can damage the surface of cards; very soft can smudge marks. Always to be kept clean and not allowed to get a dry hard skin on some types
RULERS	A straight edge with a variety of measuring marks. In many cases an actual ruler is not required but a straight edged long piece of thin wood can be excellent. The divisions marked are not in themselves important — they serve as a location for a point, so metric or imperial measures are both practical. A fresh edge of a strip of thick paper or mounting card can be used. The length should be a metre or a yard. Transparent material has advantages
RULING PEN	A pen having two parallel blades adjustable for their width apart which will carry between them a liquid — ink or water colour — and in use produce an even line. Needs considerable practice to avoid blots. Stilo tipped draughtsman pen — having a fine tube as a nib which produces an even line. A variety of line width available Excellent for non-blotting. Capable of being used with thin white water colour.
SANDPAPER	A paper covered with abrasive sand. Obtainable in varying degrees of roughness. Emery paper or cloth is similar, using corundum, and more satisfactory for use on metal.
SAW	A back (sometimes called a tennon) saw 300 mm (12 in.) blade which has teeth about 16 per 25 mm (1 in.)
SCREW EYES	A screw which has a ring at its head
SET SQUARE	Transparent plastic triangle having one 90° angle and two 45° angles
SILK SCREEN	Uses a fine material screen which in areas not required to print is blocked out. On coarse screen the dots can be seen as the ink has passed through the gaps in the weaver

SIZES

	International metric sizes	Imperial approximate equivalent
A1	841 mm x 594 mm	33 in. x 23 in.
A2	594 mm x 420 mm	23 in. x 16½ in.
A3	420 mm x 297 mm	16½ in. x 11½ in.
A4	297 mm x 210 mm	11½ in. x 8¼ in.

STRETCHER	A wooden frame on which a canvas is tacked. The corners are tongue and grooved and by the use of wedges are expandable — thus tightening the canvas
TAPE	Clear sticky tape is not so useful. Water based gum tape for use on old fragile work. Masking tape — probably one of the most useful types — paper with a mild but good sticking power

T SQUARE	A wood straight edge with a cross piece at 90° at one end
TUNGSTEN BIT	A specially tipped bit for cutting into hard brick
VICE	A metal or wood adjustable clamp, which can be fixed to a table. Wooden facing pieces should be added — most metal vices provide screw fixing holes
VIGNETTE	Not a firm rectangle but a shape made of the objects drawn. The area tends to occupy an oval
WATER COLOUR PAINTING	A painting using pigment carried in water based glue and applied in transparent or semi transparent washes allowing the paper to affect the final tones obtained
WEIGHTS	1 gm = 0.0353 oz 1 oz = 28.35 gm 1 kg = 2.2046 lb 1 lb = 0.4536 kg
WHITE SPIRIT	Double rectified paraffin sometimes called turps substitute. Excellent for it leaves no sticky resinous deposit

Suppliers

Artist's materials, including Paper, Card and Paint; Gold Leaf and Japan Gold Size	Winsor & Newton Wealdstone Harrow Middlesex HA3 5RH	**Metal edging**	Ironmongers, specialist metal suppliers; listed as Sheet Metal or Aluminium
	Berol Ltd Oldmedow Road King's Lynn Norfolk PE30 4JR	**Paper and card and frame packs**	Daler Board Co Ltd East Street Wareham Dorset BH20 4NT
	Dryad Ltd P.O. Box 38 Northgates Leicester LE1 9BU		Samuel Grant, Ltd Garnet Road Leeds LS11 5LA
		Plastic sheet	Specialist suppliers listed as Plastic Sheet
	Reeves and Sons Ltd Lincoln Road Enfield Middlesex	**Tools** including boxes and devices for cutting mitres	Ironmongers: Department stores; Specialist tool shops
	George Rowney & Co Ltd P.O. Box 10 Bracknell Berkshire RG12 4ST	**Whiting and Titanium dioxide**	Wengers Etruria Stoke on Trent Suppliers of Pottery materials; large Chemists Boots Ltd
Fillers — car type	Garages, car supply shops	**Wood**	Local wood yards listed under Timber merchants
Frame mouldings in wood	D.I.Y. Do it yourself local shops, often part of ironmongers and hardware shops		
General Artist's materials	Local art shops and Art and Craft shops		
Glass	Local glass works		
Lights	Electrical specialist shops; Department stores		

In the USA most materials are obtainable from large department stores and Do-It-Yourself shops. For the names and addresses of specialist firms consult the Yellow Pages of your telephone directories

Index

INDEX

Acknowledgment
I would like to thank Tony Birks-Hay who first suggested the
idea of this book to me; Jacqueline Yorke who, as well as typing
the script, was the 'hands' in all the photographs, and
John Mennell who gave specialist photographic assistance.